# The Wonders of Wellness

## A guide to discovering your inner calm

## Michelle Pattenden

### D.Hyp.SSOH

facebook.com/thewondersofwellness

instagram.com/thewondersofwellness

thewondersofwellness.co.uk

michelle@thewondersofwellness.co.uk

To
Luca & Arlo
Always believe in the
Magic
Love 'Chelles'

This book has been such a collaboration of
amazing ideas, artistic talent and passion.

Angie, Di, Carla, Lori and Alicia - your input
has been invaluable and I am so grateful for you!

To my family, who have believed in me every
step of the way.

To Max,
who literally brought this book to life.
I couldn't have done it without you.

# Contents

# A bit about me!

My name is Michelle Pattenden but call me 'Chelles'.

I am very lucky to live in a beautiful part of the world called Somerset. It's in the UK and is famous for its cider and Glastonbury Festival.

My journey to all things wellness began at an early age. I actually started out as an artist and was asked to deliver therapeutic art sessions to people suffering with their mental health.

That experience had such a profound effect on me. Everyone really seemed to enjoy their art time and told me in their individual ways how they were able to find peace in their minds during my sessions. And there it was, I had found my calling, I knew I wanted to heal people.

Now a practicing hypnotherapist, Reiki Master and Stress Management Therapist, I have worked to bring wellness to thousands of people, each of them teaching me something different. I hold them all in my heart as I write this book.

I feel so grateful to have been a part of their journeys and everything I do is in honour of the strength they show as they overcome their barriers and trauma whilst discovering their own unique selves that are both beautiful and magical.

I am a regular guest speaker at well-being events across the globe and am known best for sharing effective and simple mindset techniques that enable people to free their limiting beliefs and become the very best version of themselves.

My mission is to share nuggets of wellness wisdom with the world so that everyone can find calm in the chaos.

Chelles♡

Magic
is finding the *calm*
within the chaos

# Let's begin

*"When all you know is fight or flight,
red flags and butterflies all feel the same"*

Worries, fears and anxieties are something the majority of us have all experienced and they are normal reactions to stress and danger.
They can actually be very useful in keeping us safe and on track when navigating through life as they trigger the release of a hormone called adrenaline. This creates physical and emotional changes, helping us to challenge or run from dangerous situations. This response and state is more commonly known as 'fight or flight.'

However, if we permanently live in a fight or flight state, it can have a negative effect on our body and depletes it of the essential energy we need in order to maintain a healthy balance. This can
disrupt many areas of our life and well-being.

We can experience effects like sleep disturbances and our
mind can become easily distracted and fatigued, affecting our ability to make decisions or concentrate on tasks. We can become more emotional and make rash decisions or react out of proportion to events. Our body can become more susceptible to illness as our immune system
is lowered and we can often suffer from headaches and
stress-induced symptoms.

However!

Just as our body knows how to go into fight mode , it also knows how to calm us down. We can help it do this more effectively
by using different strategies to slow down the mind, and the body, and discover our own inner place of calm…

5

# Scale it   'Just for today, I will not worry'

Worrying is exhausting. It takes up so much of that valuable time that we don't seem to have and leaves us feeling mentally and physically drained.

It makes our day-to-day life feel very difficult and we have so many other amazing things that we could be getting on with.

If there is a particular worry that is really causing you issues, a way to gain back control is to scale it, with one being the calmest and 10 being the highest anxiety.

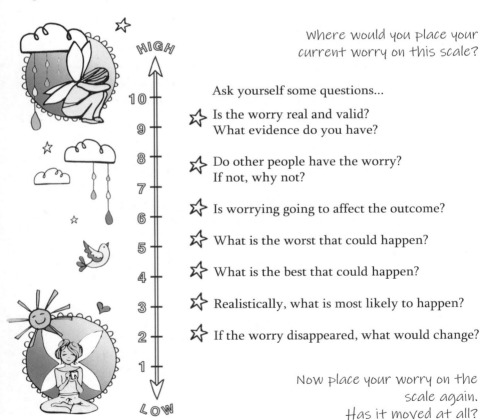

Where would you place your current worry on this scale?

Ask yourself some questions...

☆ Is the worry real and valid? What evidence do you have?

☆ Do other people have the worry? If not, why not?

☆ Is worrying going to affect the outcome?

☆ What is the worst that could happen?

☆ What is the best that could happen?

☆ Realistically, what is most likely to happen?

☆ If the worry disappeared, what would change?

Now place your worry on the scale again. Has it moved at all?

A page for my thoughts...

# Making changes

If you want to make changes to your thoughts and mindset but don't know how to begin, then making small adjustments and creating new habits physically in your daily routine is a good place to start.

We all have routines, some we are very aware of and some we are not. We tend to stick to what we know as it makes us feel safer. The more you think about it, the more surprised you may be about how much of a habit and routine you are in physically and mentally.

So where do you start? Here are some ideas to start today!
Notice how different you feel and how your emotions change.

When you get out of bed in the morning put your feet on the floor, hands on your chest, take a deep breath and say to yourself - 'Today is going to be an amazing day.'

Change items around in the kitchen. Swap complete cupboards around so the next time you instinctively go for those biscuits, because you are feeling stressed or bored, it will give you a moment to think about what you are doing and whether it is really the biscuits you need!

Sort your wardrobe. Not only will this help declutter and save space but will also help you identify what makes you feel good and what doesn't. Are there particular clothes that make you feel more confident?

Change your shampoo, shower gel, washing powder, air freshener and scented candles - new smells will revitalise your senses and start creating new memories.

Take a different route to school, work or college. Different scenery and journey times will mean that you experience new sensations and also reduce your 'autopilot' state, so that you can really appreciate what is going on around you.

Meet up or contact a friend that you haven't spoken to for a while. New conversations and outlooks can be very refreshing.

Pick a genre of film or book that you wouldn't normally watch or read. You may be surprised at what else you enjoy!

Buy a food item or drink that you haven't tasted before or find a recipe for a new meal you've never attempted before.

Making small changes will help you keep moving forward and you will find that you'll become much more mindful of everything else in your life, such as how you react to certain situations or people. Notice how you feel when changes do happen and what makes you calm.

By stepping out of your comfort zone and discovering new ways of seeing things you will begin to feel more in control when the big changes happen in your life. You'll also react differently to stressful episodes, people or triggers.

# Reframe your thoughts

*'If you always do what you've always done,
you will always get what you've always got.'*

We can change the way we think, feel and respond to stressful or overwhelming situations. We often convince ourselves that we have no control over how we feel, or that we always react and behave in a certain way. But we CAN and DO have the power to change our responses!

Try this...

Look out of the window and make a note of what you can ...

## See    Hear    Feel

❀ Now note three things that made you feel good about what you were seeing, hearing and feeling.

❀ Now note down three things that made you feel uncomfortable or unsettled about what you saw, heard or felt.

You have a choice when you look out of the window to think in two vastly different ways, yet your view is the same. The only difference between the lists are how you decide to think about them.

*This is called 'reframing' and you can do it with any situation. Whether it is at work or home, choose a situation, make those lists and change the way you choose to look at something!*

# Flip the script

Did you know that your brain doesn't know the difference between anxiety and excitement - so use this to your advantage!

Both excitement and anxiety involve the same chemical process in the brain. Anxiety is a negative experience and excitement is a positive experience.

## Write down something that triggers anxiety

For example...
"I feel anxious when I have to talk to someone I don't know.."

## Now reframe it!

Rewrite your internal script and tell yourself...
"I am excited when meeting new people .. I love the opportunity to make new friends!"

Notice how your mind and body reacts
when you flip that internal script!

# Change your perspective on a situation.

Event - Think of an event that has left you feeling unsettled.

Old Meaning - Record what you believe the event
meant to you. (This is your unhealthy belief)

New Meaning - Record a healthier and
more accurate meaning for the event.
(This is the new belief, you can work on strengthening.)

### Event

I bumped into a friend today, they hardly stopped to speak to me.

### Old Meaning

I must've done something to upset them, maybe they don't like me anymore.

### New Meaning

Maybe they were running late, or having a bad day.

### Event

### Old Meaning

### New Meaning

Event

Old Meaning

New Meaning

Event

Old Meaning

New Meaning

Event

Old Meaning

New Meaning

# Feel the feelings

When you get a 'worry' moment and you find yourself with
a head full of negative thoughts and anxiety, it can
be hard to think and find a way to change
them. You are 'thinking' your 'feelings'.

Try this and see how different you feel.

Mentally drop down into your body for a moment - now focus on
where you feel your anxiety and what it feels like. Is it in your
stomach or heavy on your shoulders?

Take a deep breath and breathe into the PHYSICAL
feeling, feel it and observe it.

Now your mind may start to battle with you and try to take back
control but keep redirecting it to your body - you can do this!

Keep taking deep breaths, whilst directing and focusing on your body.
Give yourself permission to just sit with this feeling for a moment.
Don't try to push it away or fight with it. As you do this
tell yourself that you can feel this feeling and still be okay.
Sit with it until you notice it changing and fading away.

Take a nice deep breath and adjust your body. Now let your body and
mind know what positive emotion you desire to feel and
tell yourself that is what you are feeling.

For example - I am calm. Then smile and imagine that
calmness washing over you!

You have just changed the way you respond to being overwhelmed
- congratulations!

# F.A.S.T

Have you ever felt so anxious about an interview, exam,
event or situation that it almost feels like the anxiety has become
bigger than the event itself?

Catastrophising means that we build something up to be so big in
our minds that our thoughts, feelings and reactions no longer
match the actual event.

It's the anticipation of something happening rather
than the reality that causes the anxiety.

Here is a simple formula to help you keep your feet on the ground
when being confronted with stressful or fearful situations.

**F** - Feel the Fear
Notice where the fear is sitting in your body and allow yourself to
acknowledge it for a moment. Refer back to the previous page.

**A** - Ask it some questions
Why is it here? What is it seeing? Close your eyes and let your imagination
guide you. Is it showing you attending a meeting in front of
10 people when the reality is only two people!

**S** - Scale it
Identify how high up the scale this feeling is and mentally start bringing it
down to a more manageable state. Change that image to a more realistic
picture or maybe change it to something that makes you smile or laugh!

**T** - Thank it!  Your mind works extremely hard to protect you,
but sometimes it works so hard it creates a fear that stops you
from doing what you want to do!

Did you know that it takes 90 seconds for an emotion to pass through
your body?  If you just allow yourself to acknowledge it instead of
pushing it away, you can feel the fear and still be okay!

# Chunk it

The thing about anxiety is that it gives us the overwhelming sense that we have to deal with all of our issues, all at once, all of the time!

Our mind has a very annoying way of loading everything on us so that we end up walking around feeling like the weight of the world is on our shoulders.

Spread things out so you don't feel like you are having to do 100 things all at once in the same day. Simplify and reorganise - you are in control!

A useful exercise for when you are feeling overwhelmed like this is to 'chunk' everything.

Write your worries down so your head can become clear and you can process things easier. This can help you work through exactly what you need to deal with first.

☆ What needs to be done today?
☆ What can be done tomorrow?
☆ What can wait until next week or next month?
☆ What is important to you?

You can do the same with emotional worries too. Timetable them!

Give yourself a day and time to devote exclusively to a particular issue. Write it in your diary and commit to it. You may decide to give the issue an hour or even a whole day.

Then leave it there!

You no longer have to think or carry your worries about with you as you know they will be dealt with on the dedicated day.

If any further worries pop into your head in the meantime, write them down so you can focus on them when you are ready to.

This will leave your mind clear to focus on the more positive aspects of your day and you won't feel like you are trying to juggle everything at once.

Your *calm* mind is
the ultimate weapon
against your challenges

## Anchoring

Anchoring is a term used to describe 'fixing' a good feeling so that you can use it whenever you need an added boost.

Say you want to anchor a feeling of confidence and boost your self-esteem. Think back to a time when you felt at your most confident - use your imagination and take yourself right back to that moment.

You may have to travel way back into the past, searching for those memories or it may come quite easily to you. It could be connected to work, a friend, or just a walk in the park when the sun was shining, and life felt good. Think of anything at all that holds meaning and feels good to you.

Now you have that memory in your mind.

Start to fill in the details, the colours, the people you were with, the clothes you were wearing, how it felt, any sounds, smells - every bit of detail you can imagine and remember.

As you picture this memory in your mind see and feel yourself experiencing a sense of confidence and positivity. Put your shoulders back and hold your head up high, lift your chin up and stretch out your arms.

Now you have achieved this feeling, you are ready to anchor it.

You can anchor in a few different ways. Try pressing your thumb and forefinger together, or press your tongue to the roof of your mouth. You can also push your thumb into the palm of your hand.

As you do this, feel those positive emotions of being confident and positive and use your imagination to connect the two things together.

Keep practising this so that whenever you use your anchor you immediately feel that rush of confidence and positivity washing over you.

You can anchor any desired feeling, whether it's calmness, confidence, peace or joy.

Your own inner super-power is waiting to be accessed!

# Defining anxiety and setting goals

What makes you anxious? Identify one of the main anxieties you want to work on. Be as detailed as you can.

Rate the severity of your anxiety, 0 (None) to 10 (High)

Notice how your rating changes on a daily basis.

| Anxiety trigger | eg. When I drive somewhere new I become anxious about getting lost, and often cancel my plans. |
|---|---|
| | |

| Date 06/08 | Date | Date | Date | Date |
|---|---|---|---|---|
| Rating 6 | Rating | Rating | Rating | Rating |
| Date | Date | Date | Date | Date |
| Rating | Rating | Rating | Rating | Rating |

20

Use the same format to identify the goal you'd like to achieve,
this time specifying how you'd like things to be
different in terms of your emotions and behaviour.

Rate how close you are to achieving your goal, 0 (No progress yet),
and 10 (Goal achieved)

| Goal related to anxiety | eg. To be able to drive to new places feeling calm and confident. |
| --- | --- |
| | |

| Date 10/11 | Date | Date | Date | Date |
| --- | --- | --- | --- | --- |
| Rating 7 | Rating | Rating | Rating | Rating |
| Date | Date | Date | Date | Date |
| Rating | Rating | Rating | Rating | Rating |

21

# Feeling overwhelmed?

Although it is normal to experience a level of stress or anxiety at times, for some it can become so overwhelming that it turns into a panic or anxiety attack.

Remember...
You are not the only one who has experienced this!

These can be frightening and can last from a few minutes to an hour, and have a range of symptoms from feeling faint, shortness of breath, dizziness, feeling sick, chest pain or even feeling like you are not connected to your body!

It can be exhausting and actually trigger a fear response, so you end up becoming afraid of having another one, and so the 'fear of fear' cycle can begin.

Remember...
You are NOT going crazy!

Did you know...
Human beings are programmed to deal with more than you'd think, and panic attacks are our primitive, subconscious mind's way of keeping us safe, and a natural survival response.

So what can you do if you feel panic coming on?
Here are some simple techniques you can discreetly try!

# Finger holds

The theory behind this exercise is that there is a channel of energy
connected with different organs of the body. As you hold a finger, usually
within a minute or two you will feel a throbbing or pulsing sensation.
This means that the energy is now flowing and balanced, and usually
the strong emotion will pass.

*Each finger is associated with a different emotion...*

Thumb - for tears, grief and emotional pain
Hold and breathe in peace and comfort

Index finger - for fear
Hold and breathe in courage and strength

Middle finger - for anger and rage
Hold and breathe in compassion and energy

Ring finger - for anxiety and nervousness
Hold and breathe in peace and security

Small finger - for feelings of low self esteem
Hold and breathe in gratitude and appreciation

You can use these finger holds to help feelings of panic or overwhelm. You
can also try finger holds when you are relaxing to music or just before going
to sleep, to release any tension from the day.

*Remember... If you wait - the fear will pass, if you
run away it is much more likely to keep returning.*

By using and practising the techniques in this
book you will have a 'tool box' of stratagies to use to beat anxiety.

# Taking back control

Use this sheet to take back control of
your worries and anxiety.

I am anxious because...

I am really afraid that...

This anxiety is triggering my fear of...

why do I have this fear?          How did it all start?

I am really afraid that...

The worst that can happen...

How would I cope if the worst was to happen...

The best that can happen is...

What can I do now
to ensure the most positive outcome?

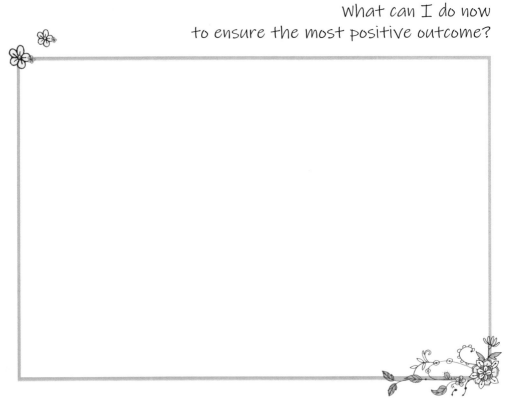

# Your inner child

Sometimes our anxieties go right back to when we were little.

Our identity and reality is heavily influenced by experiences and interactions we had as a child, and the voices of the adults around us. Maybe that's why, when we are adults, we revert back to those old insecurities about feeling different or not good enough. Our responses are those of our 'inner child.'

However - we do have the power to change those old anxious thoughts!

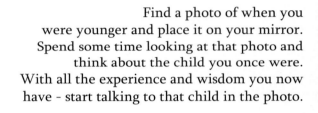

Find a photo of when you were younger and place it on your mirror. Spend some time looking at that photo and think about the child you once were. With all the experience and wisdom you now have - start talking to that child in the photo.

Tell them how well they have done to survive! Tell them that although they may make mistakes, you will love and look after them.

Tell them everything they need to hear and talk to them as you would any other child. Forgive them of everything and remove any guilt or responsibility they may be feeling as you understand - with your older mind - that as a child they hold no blame.

Tell them that they are beautiful, intelligent, good and kind, and make a promise to continue to look after them in body and mind.

Keep that photo up and every morning when you are getting ready, send some good thoughts and love to your inner child. The one that needs looking after and protecting and as you notice your inner child starting to feel loved and valued, YOU will start to value and respect yourself and feel more in control.

Every day... look after this child. Look after the inner you!

# Send a message

In times of high anxiety, we
can forget just how powerful our
own voice can be - just as we listen
to our negative self-talk, we can
combat this by sending some
positive feel-good talk back!

Write yourself a letter, record yourself a voice
message or video full of wisdom, love and reminders
that any negative feelings you are experiencing at
the moment are not permanent.

When something happens that makes you feel good or
you are just feeling calm and relaxed, then record it so you
can listen to it at a later date.

Give yourself little snippets of advice (nuggets of wisdom).
If you read something or discover a technique that would be
useful to you when you're stressed, record or write it down.

Create your own well-being journal or voice message file to build
up a toolkit of self-support and encouragement.

Become your own best friend!

Then on those days when you are feeling overwhelmed
or struggling to remember what it feels like to be calm
or happy, read or play those messages back to yourself and
you will hear how calm and in control you sound.

We forget that our own thoughts and feelings are temporary
and to read our own words or hear our own voice sounding so
positive is a powerful way of changing our mindset.

Believe it because you sent it!

Your own free, feel good therapy.

# Language

The words we use to talk to the people around us and the way we talk to ourselves has a massive effect on our sense of identity. What we tell ourselves, the deeper mind will believe, so take some time to listen to what your inner voice is saying and be mindful of the words we use.

Are you using phrases like - 'I'm not good enough.' 'I'm rubbish.' 'Nobody likes me.'
Does this sound familiar?
Would you talk like that to a child? Would you tell them that they are not good enough? I will assume you are shaking your head!

So how do you stop negative thoughts and phrases?

Start replacing the negative words with positive words. It may be hard at first. After all, this may be a whole new language pattern for you however the more you keep doing it the more your mind will start to believe you.

Write some positive thoughts

28

# However...

This is such a little word, but it can have such a profound influence on the way we respond to our inner voice. Language is so important, and it's something many of us don't take much notice of.
Have you ever stopped to notice how you describe or talk about yourself, whether it's out loud or in your head?

Things like...
'I'm broken.' 'I'm an anxious person.' 'I'm always unlucky.' 'No one likes me.'
'I'm out of control.' 'I'm ugly.'

The more you repeat these negative affirmations, the more they stick and shape the way you see yourself and the world around you.

Why? Because statements like these have a full stop. You are stating something you believe about yourself and reinforcing it, which gives your mind no option but to carry on believing it!

 ## Now add that word 'However'

 I'm broken, HOWEVER... I'm working on healing myself.

I'm anxious, HOWEVER... I know this feeling is temporary.

I'm depressed, HOWEVER... I am going to get through today.

I'm full of negative thoughts, HOWEVER... I know they are just thoughts.

I feel like I can't do it, HOWEVER... I'm going to find a way.

Be mindful of the statements you are feeding yourself. Have a think about the language you are using and use 'however' to open that door to release the negative trap and find solutions.

You really can make a difference to your mindset
and well-being by taking this small step.

29

'What if' statements

What if I fail?

Write down your most self-reinforcing 'What If' Statements. Transform those negative 'What if's' into positive statements.

30

Positive
statements

What if I succeed?

Things to remember...

In the midst of
movement and chaos,
keep *stillness* inside
of you

# Just for a moment

If you stop for a moment
and step inside your heart,
you may just feel the magic
of a calm about to start.

If you breathe for a moment
and drop into your soul,
you may just release something
that's been taking it's toll.

If you listen for a moment,
you may just start to hear
a voice that says 'I Love You'
as it begins to venture near.

If you feel for a moment
and realise you're still okay,
that burden you were carrying
will start to fade away.

Chelles♡

# Meditation

Meditation gives the body and mind time to reconnect and relax. It slows everything down and can help to reduce anxiety and panic attacks.
It can also help with sleep issues and to achieve clarity of mind, giving you the time and space to process what is going on around you.

There are many different types of meditation but I'm going to focus on micro-meditations which can be easily incorporated into your day and take no longer than five to 15 minutes. The more often you practice them, the easier and more natural they become.
There is no right or wrong way of meditating - the purpose is to direct your focus and attention to what is going on in your mind and body at that moment in time.

*Tip* - Put a timer on your phone starting at one to two minutes and build the time up gradually. It's surprising just how little time we spend focusing purely on ourselves in a loving, mindful way.

Five minutes in the outside world can speed by, however five minutes of focusing on yourself can feel like a significant amount of time!

Many people find it easier and more enjoyable to practice guided meditation. If you think this would help you, and you'd like to hear my voice, visit thewondersofwellness.co.uk

Breathe

# And relaaaaaaaax......

Conscious relaxation is the ability to relax your body and mind completely - without falling asleep!
We store so much tension in our body, giving us aching shoulders, headaches and tight stomachs. Every stressful and negative emotion gets stored within our body and mind unless we find a way to release it.

Take 10 mins out of your day to try this muscle relaxation exercise either before you get out of bed in the morning or before you go to sleep.

Take a slow deep breath in and out, exhaling out as far as you can.

Turn your attention to your forehead and tense those tiny muscles that are storing all the tension, hold it for a few moments.

On your next breath out... relax those muscles, and feel the tension flowing away.

Turn your attention to your jaw, tense it and grit your teeth.

On your next breath out... relax the jaw and let your tongue go limp.

Focus next on your shoulders, bringing them up to your ears and tensing them tight.

Breathe out... let your shoulders drop down loose and relaxed.

Tense the muscles on either side of your spine and feel that tension.

As you breathe out... feel that relaxation flowing in as you sink deeper into your bed.

Continue to tense and relax the muscles throughout your body, observing the differences.

37

# Micro-sense

Micro meditiation while you shower.

A perfect time to micro-meditate is when you are
in the shower - you can use mindfulness to enhance
your senses whilst getting ready for the day or before
you go to bed.

Make sure you are standing with your feet placed
at a comfortable distance apart and close your eyes.
Take some deep breaths and start to use all
of your senses.

*SMELL* the shampoo and soap.

*FEEL* the sensation of the water on your body.

*OBSERVE* the temperature of the water.

*NOTICE* the feeling of the
shower tray beneath your feet.

*LISTEN* to the sound of the water
and any other sounds you hear.

Open your eyes and *WATCH* how the
water droplets run down your arm.

*TASTE* the water on your tongue.

# Micro-grounding

### Micro meditation while boiling the kettle.

In the time it takes for the kettle to boil, you can centre, ground and
rebalance yourself. Once the cups are out and the kettle is boiling,
stand with your feet at a comfortable distance apart and
close your eyes. Take some deep breaths and imagine your entire
body filled up with water, like a water dispenser in an office or gym.

Now, imagine there is a tap on your ankle. Undo that tap and visualise
the water beginning to drain out of you and
into the ground. Imagine the flow of energy through
your body and feel your feet firmly on the ground.

Feel free to continue this meditation for as long
as the kettle takes to boil.

# Micro-mindfulness

Spending time outside is a highly effective way to relieve anxiety and ground yourself.

This is a lovely meditation to do whilst you are out walking.

Take a moment to notice the speed at which you are walking and how you are breathing.

Are you rushing and shallow breathing?
Can you slow your pace down for a few minutes?
Find a nice steady pace that suits you.

Now, imagine that you are seeing everything for the very first time... really notice the colour of the leaves on the trees and the different shades of the buildings and brickwork.

Look right up to the tops of the buildings - the bits we never notice when we are rushing to our next destination.

Notice how hard or soft the ground feels beneath your feet.
Listen to the sound of each step that you take and the other different noises you can hear. How many are loud and how many are in the distance.

Loosen your shoulders and unclench your hands and jaw.
Breathe in and enjoy the fresh air with all its different smells.

As you walk, for just a few minutes, do not think of anything but that moment in time.

See, feel and sense the beauty in the environment you are in and your pace within it. Notice how connected and grounded you feel now.

# Micro-relaxation

You can do this meditation whilst sitting in the
office, sitting on the sofa or on the bus!

Start by taking a few slow deep *breaths* either
closing your eyes or if you feel more comfortable, keep them open.

*Imagine* a wave of golden energy flowing down from the top of your
head and sliding down your scalp.

*Tilt* your chin up a bit as if you were basking
in the warmth of the sun on your face.

*Imagine* yourself breathing in relaxation and breathing out tension,
with every breath imagine your muscles unwinding and relaxing.

*Feel* your heartbeat slowing down, and your
body becoming heavier, sinking into the chair.

*Breathe* in and out deeply and slowly for a few minutes,
imagining that golden energy filling every part
of your body as you sense all your tension melting away.

Now, *imagine* your body becoming lighter and lighter again
as you become more aware of the outside world around you.

*Stretch* your arms and *smile* - you are
now ready to continue on with your day!

# Take a breath

There are many different breathing techniques and they can all be remarkably effective in changing your physical and emotional state.

It seems so simple - after all - breathing is something we do all the time! However, in a state of high anxiety we often shallow breathe which can have a negative impact on our body.

Here are two simple techniques that can help create a state of calm extremely quickly.

## Focus on the out breath

Breathe in through your nose normally then on the out breath, imagine you are blowing up a balloon and send that out breath as far as you can, for as long as you can, then close your mouth as you breathe in again through your nose.

On the out breath, notice your body relaxing and tension being released.

## Double breath sigh

Take a breath in and before you breathe out take ANOTHER breath in again. Then breathe out with a big sigh.

You may have seen babies do this when they are calming down from crying - it's the body's way of naturally relieving stress. You will often feel a significant calming effect from the first attempt of this.

# Inner calm statements

I allow myself to feel this way and still be okay

I choose to slow down, and breathe

I'm stronger than I give myself credit for

Anxiety is normal and I am using my coping strategies

I stay present and ground myself

I always survive this

I have everything I need to get through this

My thoughts are just thoughts and they will pass

I focus on my breathing in this moment

I tune into my body and release tension from my muscles

Be gentle with yourself, you're doing the best you can

You are
strong enough to
*face it all*, even
if it doesn't feel
like it right
now

# Things that make me calm...

# Sleep easily

Many people struggle with maintaining consistent healthy sleep patterns and it can become worse when you are feeling anxious or stressed. Sleep can be affected in different ways, either you lose sleep through worrying or sleep too much due to exhaustion, you may wake up many times in the night or have vivid unsettling dreams.

It can be quite easy to slip into a cycle of convincing yourself that you cannot sleep, that you are going to wake up in the night and be tired in the morning. What you are then doing is reinforcing the inner belief that you can't sleep, which in turn can actually stop you from falling asleep.

Try turning your thoughts around and start telling yourself this...

I CAN fall asleep easily.
I CAN go back to sleep if I wake up.
I CAN sleep peacefully.
I CAN deal with everything else tomorrow.
I CAN SLEEP!

Having a good sleep routine is vital to creating a good foundation to preparing to sleep well.

Try and avoid daytime naps if you are waking up frequently during the night. Avoid staying in bed too long in the mornings and set the alarm to get up at the same time every day.

Avoid lying in bed awake - get up and read a book for a while, fold up some laundry or practise some meditation until you feel tired again, but don't go online!

Avoid too much caffeine in the evening, it can stay in your system for a very long time. There are many natural herbal drinks that can help promote sleep.

Ensure that your bedroom is a cosy, quiet place to be, somewhere you associate with relaxation and rest.

If you would like more help with sleeping, visit wondersofwellness.co.uk

When you fall asleep tonight, I want you to
think of at least one thing that has been good today.
It might be difficult and you may think there is nothing;
but however bad a day has been, there is always one thing,
even if it's a tiny thing, that has been good,
and sometimes it can be helpful to remind
yourself of that as you fall asleep.

'Sleep is a golden thread that ties
our health and bodies together.'

# Keep smiling

*'Today I am going to smile with my eyes!'*

Did you know that it takes three times as much energy and at least double the amount of muscles to frown rather than smile?

It is also a fact that our well-being is influenced by our facial expressions.

When we smile it helps to uplift our brain fluctuations and our mental attitudes. Even if we don't feel like smiling as soon as we do the effects are still the same! It's like our secret 'feel good' trick. Also, the more we smile, the better we get at it!

A sense of humour helps us balance out our lives and without it, we tend to slip into a pattern of negative or depressing thoughts.

Having a good laugh can help us free our minds and relax our muscles as well as expressing our voice and increasing our energy levels.

Think back to the last time YOU smiled and laughed… Now go and look in the mirror and give yourself a smile. Focus on smiling until it reaches your eyes. Observe any differences in your body when you smile.

Now smile at someone else and watch their reaction. Smiling can become very contagious!

# Gut health

Our gut health often gets overlooked in its impact on emotional health.

It's a fact that physically you must eat the right foods otherwise your body can feel sluggish, gain weight and increase your risk of disease. But have you ever thought about how food can affect your mental health?

Sugar - fluctuations in blood sugar can change your mood - too high and you can end up feeling irritable and restless and too low can make you feel anxious and depressed.

Vitamins - vitamins can help boost SEROTONIN. Serotonin is our HAPPINESS chemical and although it is manufactured in our brains, 90% of our serotonin supply is found in our digestive tract. Low levels of vitamins, mineral deficiencies and low intake of fatty acids and omega-3's can affect mood and actually mimic mental health issues. Insufficient levels of vitamin D can lead to mood swings, depression and fatigue.

Foods that are NOT GOOD for your mental health! - sugary drinks, refined carbs, trans fats foods, highly processed foods, aspartame, alcohol, fish high in mercury.

Foods that are GOOD for your mental health! - fatty fish, blueberries, turmeric, broccoli, pumpkin seeds, dark chocolate, nuts, oranges, eggs, green tea.

Allergies and intolerances like dairy and gluten can have a big effect on your mood and can leave you feeling sluggish and unmotivated.

Try keeping a food diary to explore how food may be affecting your moods, you may be surprised to notice a pattern.

By focusing on your mental health diet, you could find that you start feeling more energetic, motivated, calmer and less anxious. This in turn may encourage you to increase the amount of exercise you take and open up opportunities of living a healthier lifestyle to benefit you emotionally and physically.

# Get moving

Our mental health responds well to physical activities.
Exercise is a natural and effective anti-anxiety treatment!

It relieves tension and stress, boosts physical and mental energy and enhances well-being through the release of endorphins. These endorphins also help you to concentrate and feel mentally sharp.

Moving your body stimulates the growth of new brain cells and helps prevent age related decline. When you feel good about doing some exercise it boosts your self-esteem and gives you a sense of self-worth, making you feel strong and powerful. The more times you increase your heart rate the more energy and motivation you will feel.

Some good for the mind, subtle body exercises
are stretching, Tai Chi and Yoga.

You don't need to be super fit, bendy or a certain shape or age to enjoy these types of exercises and they are ideal ways of reducing tension without being competitive. Subtle body exercises affect emotional well-being in a much deeper way and allow the mind to achieve clarity and insight. They work from the inside out and focus on fluidity, concentration and meditation. They create movement that promotes inner harmony and well-being.

You can do a few stretches before you get out of bed in the morning to wake yourself up or before you go to sleep at night to wind down. Incorporate them with some simple breathing and meditation techniques. This is a great way of grounding and releasing tension and stress.

Take a breath and write your thoughts

# Gratitude ♡

*'The quality of being thankful. The readiness
to show appreciation and returning kindness'*

Gratitude is a way to appreciate what you have instead of focusing
on what you don't. It helps you to refocus on the here and now instead
of always reaching for something new in the hope that it will
make you happier.

Studies have found that regularly expressing gratitude can
help you feel more positive, improve health, deal with adversity and
build new relationships.

## Ways to express gratitude

Send a thank you to someone. Make a habit of sending a thank you
note once a month to show appreciation of that person's impact on your
life and every now and again - send one to yourself!

Write a list of things you are grateful for every day.
Challenge yourself to find things you are grateful for particularly on
those tough days and as you write, be specific and as detailed as you can
about what exactly you are feeling grateful for.

Meditate - mindfulness meditation means focusing on the present
moment without judgement. You could focus on one word
like 'calm' or 'peace' and what you are grateful for.  For example, the
warmth of the sun, a pleasant walk, friends and family etc…

# Benefits of gratitude

1. Strengthens resiliency

2. Reduces depression

3. Reduces feelings of jealousy

4. Improves physical health

5. Retain more positive experiences

6. Less chronic pain

7. Increases energy levels

8. Increases self-esteem

9. More inclined to help others

10. Improves sleep

'I'm so grateful for you!'

# Morning gratitude thoughts

Before you begin your day, write 10 things you're grateful for (big or small)

1.

2.

3.

4.

5.

6.

7.

8.

9.

10.

# The best part of my day

Choose one moment of your day that made you happy, and focus on it for 5 minutes before you go to sleep

# What I'm learning from my challenges

List three challenges situations, people, or other obstacles

1. I'm learning...

2. I'm learning...

3. I'm learning...

# People I'm thankful for

List five people who made your life a little happier today. They could be friends, family or even strangers!

1.

2.

3.

4.

5.

# Building a support network

'Call it a clan, call it a network, call it a tribe, call it a family, whatever you call it, whoever you are, you need one.'

**Find at least one support person in each area of your life**

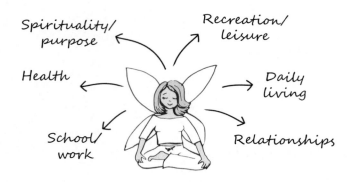

Spirituality/
purpose

Recreation/
leisure

Health

Daily
living

School/
work

Relationships

## Support People:

Name:                                   Contact:

1.

2.

3.

4.

5.

6.

Make sure these people are in your phone contact lists!

# Time to pause...
### and take some notes

# Self love ♡

When a baby is shown love, they accept it with no hesitation -
it is the most natural and instinctive thing to do. But somehow as we
grow up, we seem to find it harder and harder to accept love and most
importantly, love ourselves.

Without self-love we create a reality for ourselves where we never
feel 'good enough.' It's only once we start to feel worthy and value
ourselves, that we can begin to send the messages and energy that
our body and soul needs to hear to make the changes required.

Every day, no matter how strange it feels,
take a moment to look in the mirror and say:

## 'I love you'

Even if you don't believe it to begin with, just start.
Even if you don't feel it to begin with, just do it. ♡

Give yourself permission to love yourself and send that
love right back to your younger self.

To heal -
You must first accept yourself.

To move on -
You must first forgive yourself.

To create calm -
You must first acknowledge yourself.

To create change -
You must first love yourself.

If you love, respect and value yourself, your energy will radiate
and start touching the people around you.

Self-love frees you from the limiting beliefs you have carried
around, and creates the foundations you need to release fear and
anxiety in order to discover your inner calm.

'I see you in all your beauty and excellence, so
that your light will one day shine so bright
even you will see your magic.'

## Searching for calm

I searched as far as I could see,
I looked in between the trees,
I delved deep into the forest,
until I fell onto my knees.

I stared up to the stars,
looking beyond the distant sky.
I lost myself in the abyss
not knowing if I could fly.

I dived into the ocean,
allowing the tide to sweep me away.
I searched within the caverns below
but found I couldn't stay.

I sent my energy outwards,
searching for the hidden key
that would starve the anxiety gremlin
and finally set me free.

But then I stopped and took a pause
and started searching deep inside,
to the stars and beauty already within
and I realised the gremlin had lied.

I already had the key,
I just hadn't known where to look.
I never believed that I could be enough
to get back what the gremlin took.

And as I started to embrace
the magic and the light that was me,
calmness found it's way through
and I finally began to see.

And I started to understand
that my power came from within,
calmness became stronger still
and the gremlin began to dim.

My journey brought me back home.
I fell in love with the person who shone.
No matter what challenges lay ahead
my strength, my calm, has won.

Chelles♡

*time to doodle*

Sometimes it's okay
if the only thing
you did today was
*breathe*

My Positive Affirmation: _____

| | Monday | Tuesday | Wednesday | Thursday | Friday | Saturday | Sunday |
|---|---|---|---|---|---|---|---|
| What am I grateful for? | | | | | | | |
| What went well today? | | | | | | | |
| How can I improve? | | | | | | | |
| What have I overcome? | | | | | | | |
| Anxiety rating 0-10 | | | | | | | |

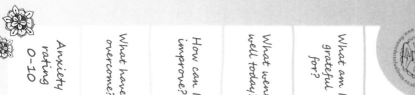

My Positive Affirmation:

| | Monday | Tuesday | Wednesday | Thursday | Friday | Saturday | Sunday |
|---|---|---|---|---|---|---|---|
| What am I grateful for? | | | | | | | |
| What went well today? | | | | | | | |
| How can I improve? | | | | | | | |
| What have I overcome? | | | | | | | |
| Anxiety rating 0-10 | | | | | | | |

# Extra support

## Anxiety
anxietyuk.org.uk
supportline.org.uk
socialanxietysupport.com

## Counselling
britishpsychotherapyfoundation.org.uk
counselling-directory.org.uk

## Mental Health
mentalhealth.org.uk
mind.org.uk
moodscope.com
rcpsych.ac.uk
rethink.org
actionforhappiness.org
sane.org.uk
time-to-change.org.uk
samaritans.org

## General Health
bupa.co.uk
childline.org.uk
netdoctor.co.uk
nhs.uk
patient.co.uk

**Addiction** - alcoholic-anonymous.org.uk
ukna.org
**Alzheimer's** - alzheimers.org.uk
**Bereavement** - cruse.org.uk
**Depression** - depressionalliance.org;
**PTSD** - www.ptsduk.org
**Suicide** - metanoia.org

For more help with mental health / anxiety
please visit thewondersofwellness.co.uk

66

There is no greater
wealth in this world than
*peace of mind*

# wellness

/ˈwelnes/

## noun

the act of practicing healthy habits on a daily basis to attain better, physical, and mental health outcomes, so that instead of just surviving...

you're thriving.

BV - #0115 - 100521 - C74 - 210/148/4 - PB - 9781914195440 - Matt Lamination